THE ROYAL
HORTICULTURAL
SOCIETY

DIARY
2019

F FRANCES
LINCOLN

First published in 2018 by Frances Lincoln,
an imprint of the Quarto Group
The Old Brewery, 6 Blundell Street,
London N7 9BH, United Kingdom
www.QuartoKnows.com

A catalogue record for this book is
available from the British Library

Designed by Sarah Allberrey

ISBN: 978-0-7112-3948-7

Printed in China

9 8 7 6 5 4 3 2 1

Title page Watercolour on paper of *Rosa moschata*
or musk rose, painted in Shimla, India, May 1934.
Below Watercolour of *Tecoma capensis* or Cape
honeysuckle, painted in Madras, India, 1931.

RHS FLOWER SHOWS 2019
The Royal Horticultural Society holds a number
of prestigious flower shows throughout the year.
At the time of going to press, show dates for 2019
had not been confirmed but details can be found
on the website at: rhs.org.uk/shows-events

Every effort is made to ensure calendarial data
is correct at the time of going to press but the
publisher cannot accept any liability for any
errors or changes.

CALENDAR 2019

JANUARY
```
M  T  W  T  F  S  S
      1  2  3  4  5  6
 7  8  9 10 11 12 13
14 15 16 17 18 19 20
21 22 23 24 25 26 27
28 29 30 31
```

FEBRUARY
```
M  T  W  T  F  S  S
               1  2  3
 4  5  6  7  8  9 10
11 12 13 14 15 16 17
18 19 20 21 22 23 24
25 26 27 28
```

MARCH
```
M  T  W  T  F  S  S
               1  2  3
 4  5  6  7  8  9 10
11 12 13 14 15 16 17
18 19 20 21 22 23 24
25 26 27 28 29 30 31
```

APRIL
```
M  T  W  T  F  S  S
 1  2  3  4  5  6  7
 8  9 10 11 12 13 14
15 16 17 18 19 20 21
22 23 24 25 26 27 28
29 30
```

MAY
```
M  T  W  T  F  S  S
       1  2  3  4  5
 6  7  8  9 10 11 12
13 14 15 16 17 18 19
20 21 22 23 24 25 26
27 28 29 30 31
```

JUNE
```
M  T  W  T  F  S  S
                  1  2
 3  4  5  6  7  8  9
10 11 12 13 14 15 16
17 18 19 20 21 22 23
24 25 26 27 28 29 30
```

JULY
```
M  T  W  T  F  S  S
 1  2  3  4  5  6  7
 8  9 10 11 12 13 14
15 16 17 18 19 20 21
22 23 24 25 26 27 28
29 30 31
```

AUGUST
```
M  T  W  T  F  S  S
          1  2  3  4
 5  6  7  8  9 10 11
12 13 14 15 16 17 18
19 20 21 22 23 24 25
26 27 28 29 30 31
```

SEPTEMBER
```
M  T  W  T  F  S  S
                     1
 2  3  4  5  6  7  8
 9 10 11 12 13 14 15
16 17 18 19 20 21 22
23 24 25 26 27 28 29
30
```

OCTOBER
```
M  T  W  T  F  S  S
    1  2  3  4  5  6
 7  8  9 10 11 12 13
14 15 16 17 18 19 20
21 22 23 24 25 26 27
28 29 30 31
```

NOVEMBER
```
M  T  W  T  F  S  S
               1  2  3
 4  5  6  7  8  9 10
11 12 13 14 15 16 17
18 19 20 21 22 23 24
25 26 27 28 29 30
```

DECEMBER
```
M  T  W  T  F  S  S
                     1
 2  3  4  5  6  7  8
 9 10 11 12 13 14 15
16 17 18 19 20 21 22
23 24 25 26 27 28 29
30 31
```

CALENDAR 2020

JANUARY
```
M  T  W  T  F  S  S
       1  2  3  4  5
 6  7  8  9 10 11 12
13 14 15 16 17 18 19
20 21 22 23 24 25 26
27 28 29 30 31
```

FEBRUARY
```
M  T  W  T  F  S  S
                  1  2
 3  4  5  6  7  8  9
10 11 12 13 14 15 16
17 18 19 20 21 22 23
24 25 26 27 28 29
```

MARCH
```
M  T  W  T  F  S  S
                     1
 2  3  4  5  6  7  8
 9 10 11 12 13 14 15
16 17 18 19 20 21 22
23 24 25 26 27 28 29
30 31
```

APRIL
```
M  T  W  T  F  S  S
       1  2  3  4  5
 6  7  8  9 10 11 12
13 14 15 16 17 18 19
20 21 22 23 24 25 26
27 28 29 30
```

MAY
```
M  T  W  T  F  S  S
               1  2  3
 4  5  6  7  8  9 10
11 12 13 14 15 16 17
18 19 20 21 22 23 24
25 26 27 28 29 30 31
```

JUNE
```
M  T  W  T  F  S  S
 1  2  3  4  5  6  7
 8  9 10 11 12 13 14
15 16 17 18 19 20 21
22 23 24 25 26 27 28
29 30
```

JULY
```
M  T  W  T  F  S  S
       1  2  3  4  5
 6  7  8  9 10 11 12
13 14 15 16 17 18 19
20 21 22 23 24 25 26
27 28 29 30 31
```

AUGUST
```
M  T  W  T  F  S  S
                  1  2
 3  4  5  6  7  8  9
10 11 12 13 14 15 16
17 18 19 20 21 22 23
24 25 26 27 28 29 30
31
```

SEPTEMBER
```
M  T  W  T  F  S  S
    1  2  3  4  5  6
 7  8  9 10 11 12 13
14 15 16 17 18 19 20
21 22 23 24 25 26 27
28 29 30
```

OCTOBER
```
M  T  W  T  F  S  S
          1  2  3  4
 5  6  7  8  9 10 11
12 13 14 15 16 17 18
19 20 21 22 23 24 25
26 27 28 29 30 31
```

NOVEMBER
```
M  T  W  T  F  S  S
                     1
 2  3  4  5  6  7  8
 9 10 11 12 13 14 15
16 17 18 19 20 21 22
23 24 25 26 27 28 29
30
```

DECEMBER
```
M  T  W  T  F  S  S
    1  2  3  4  5  6
 7  8  9 10 11 12 13
14 15 16 17 18 19 20
21 22 23 24 25 26 27
28 29 30 31
```

INTRODUCTION

Lady Beatrix Stanley was an accomplished gardener and artist. She spent five years living in India with her husband, Sir George Stanley, Governor of Madras from 1929 to 1934, and Viceroy and Acting Governor-General of India in 1934. Born the youngest daughter of the Marquees of Headfort in 1877, she inherited a love of plants and gardening. 'She was able to grow, propagate and distribute plants which baffled others,' and was generous with both her knowledge and skill, sharing unusual plants with other enthusiasts. The works reproduced here are a sample of the extensive collection of paintings she produced during her time in India.

Whilst living in Madras (now Chennai), Lady Beatrix was a keen observer of gardening practices in all the places she visited. Having left behind a wonderful garden in England, she sought to create a beautiful idyll in their new home. The couple's residence was in the south, in Ootacamund, or 'Ooty' for short, but there were plenty of opportunities to travel to the north, and she wrote with enthusiasm of the gardens in Agra and New Delhi. She had a passion for growing both her beloved plants from home as well as tropical varieties. She recommended that British gardeners in India should not try too hard to replicate an English garden, as lovely as it was to be reminded of home, but seek to embrace the native shrubs and creepers that she herself found interesting.

Already established as a horticultural authority, Lady Beatrix had developed an extensive knowledge of bulbous plants with her own collection in her garden at Sibbertoft Manor, Market Harborough in Leicestershire. Edward Augustus Bowles, an expert on crocuses (amongst various other horticultural accolades), records a visit by her to Myddleton House in February 1922 to view newly flowering varieties of crocuses and snowdrops. 'Aunt B', as she was affectionately known, was counted amongst his 'plant-hunting friends', having been in the party that travelled with Bowles to the Pyrenees in 1928. Whilst in India, Bowles and Lady Beatrix maintained weekly correspondence, with seeds from new plants being sent along with observations and photographs of her travels. Much of this correspondence survives in the RHS Archives. (E.A. Bowles Archives held by the RHS Lindley Library.)

There is unfortunately no record of where our artist learnt to paint, although it seems she may have been largely self-taught. Lady Beatrix's interest in using watercolours developed whilst she was in India, and she completed over 150 pictures of plants growing in and around the gardens she visited. In her letters to Bowles in 1931 she expresses concern at the quality of her painting, particularly in the composition of floral groups. She was keen to receive feedback and sent samples of her artwork to Myddleton House from Madras. Her loose painterly style, quite common of flower painters during the period, bears some similarity to that of Bowles. She need not have been worried, as her flower paintings were exhibited at the Chelsea Flower Show in 1930 and 1931, and on both occasions she was awarded a Silver-gilt Grenfell medal.

Bold and vibrant in style, these paintings are the work of a keen and dedicated plantswoman. They provide us with a fascinating insight into Lady Stanley's horticultural world as she diligently noted genus and species, locations and dates of the plants she painted. Seeking to portray her specimens with botanical accuracy, she clearly intended these works to be a record of her time in India.

Her time there was spent not just painting and gardening, but also fostering community relations. Lady Beatrix was the president of the Nilgiri Ladies' Club, based in Ootacamund, established in 1930 to promote social intercourse between Indian and European Women. In 1935 she was awarded the Imperial Order of the Crown of India (CI), a title only conferred to women, in recognition of her time spent in India.

On her return to England, Lady Beatrix immersed herself back in the world of British horticulture with long-established friends. She had been writing short essays and notes during her time overseas and returned to work on RHS committees. Following an article for the *RHS Lily Year Book* in 1935, she was appointed editor of *The New Flora and Sylva*, between 1938 and 1940.

She is honoured in the naming of two cultivated varieties: *Iris histrioides* 'Lady Beatrix Stanley' and *Galanthus* 'Lady Beatrix Stanley'.

DECEMBER/JANUARY

---

31 *Monday*   New Year's Eve

---

01 *Tuesday*   New Year's Day
Holiday, UK, Republic of Ireland, USA,
Canada, Australia and New Zealand

---

02 *Wednesday*   Holiday, Scotland and New Zealand

---

03 *Thursday*

---

04 *Friday*

---

05 *Saturday*

---

06 *Sunday*   *New moon*
Epiphany

Watercolour of *Argyreia*, painted in India, c1930.

JANUARY

Monday 07

Tuesday 08

Wednesday 09

Thursday 10

Friday 11

Saturday 12

Sunday 13

Watercolour of *Senna siamea*, formerly known as *Cassia siamea glauca*, painted in India, c1930.

JANUARY

---

14 Monday   *First quarter*

---

15 Tuesday

---

16 Wednesday

---

17 Thursday

---

18 Friday

---

19 Saturday

---

20 Sunday

Watercolour of *Habenaria longicornu* or long-horned habenaria. An orchid native to India, it was painted showing its natural habitat in India, c1930.

Tacsonia tubiflora rosea

JANUARY

Full moon
Holiday, USA (Martin Luther King Jnr Day)

Monday 21

Tuesday 22

Wednesday 23

Thursday 24

Friday 25

Australia Day

Saturday 26

Last quarter

Sunday 27

Watercolour of *Tacsonia tubiflora rosea*, now believed to be *Passiflora mollissima*, painted in Ootacamund, India, c1930.

JANUARY/FEBRUARY

---

28 Monday

Arm's Reach Lindsay

---

29 Tuesday

Kelsey for credit card

---

30 Wednesday

House cleaning 3pm

---

31 Thursday

---

01 Friday

---

02 Saturday

---

03 Sunday

Watercolour of a pink *Hibiscus*, painted in Madras, India, in 1930.

FEBRUARY

New moon

Monday 04

Chinese New Year

Tuesday 05

Accession of Queen Elizabeth II
Holiday, New Zealand (Waitangi Day)

Wednesday 06

Thursday 07

Friday 08

Saturday 09

Sunday 10

Watercolour of a *Hibiscus*, painted in India, c1930.

FEBRUARY

11 Monday

12 Tuesday   *First quarter*

13 Wednesday

14 Thursday   Valentine's Day

15 Friday

16 Saturday

17 Sunday

Watercolour of *Ipomoea indica* or blue dawn flower, previously known as *Ipomoea learii*.
Painted in India, c1930.

Ipomoea Learii.
Leari

B.S.

FEBRUARY

Holiday, USA (Presidents' Day)

Monday 18

Full moon

Tuesday 19

Wednesday 20

Thursday 21

Friday 22

Saturday 23

Sunday 24

Watercolour on paper of *Watsonia pillansii* or Beatrice watsonia, previously known as *Watsonia beatricis*. Painted in Ootacamund, where Beatrix Stanley was in residence in southern India, in 1934.

FEBRUARY/MARCH

25 Monday

26 Tuesday   *Last quarter*

27 Wednesday

28 Thursday

01 Friday   St David's Day

02 Saturday

03 Sunday

Watercolour of *Tabebuia rosea* or pink trumpet tree, previously known as *Tecoma rosea*.
Painted in Ootacamund, India, c1930.

MARCH

Monday 04

Shrove Tuesday

Tuesday 05

New moon
Ash Wednesday

Wednesday 06

Thursday 07

Friday 08

Saturday 09

Sunday 10

Watercolour on paper of *Cornus capitata*, the Himalayan evergreen dogwood. Painted in Shimla in the Himalayan foothills, India, 1934.

MARCH

11 Monday   Commonwealth Day

12 Tuesday

13 Wednesday

14 Thursday   First quarter

15 Friday

16 Saturday

17 Sunday   St Patrick's Day

Watercolour of *Memecylon umbellatum* or iron wood tree, painted in India, c1930.
The inscription by the artist reads: 'From plant brought in from jungle by
Capt. Bootle Wilbraham', the Governor's Military Secretary.

Holiday, Northern Ireland and Republic
of Ireland (St Patrick's Day)

Elaine to San José Monday 18

Tuesday 19

Vernal Equinox (Spring begins)

Wednesday 20

Full moon

Thursday 21

Friday 22

Saturday 23

Sunday 24

Watercolour of *Tristellateia australasiae*, painted in India, c1930.

25 *Monday*

26 *Tuesday*

27 *Wednesday*

28 *Thursday*   *Last quarter*

29 *Friday*

30 *Saturday*

31 *Sunday*   Mothering Sunday, UK and Republic of Ireland
British Summer Time begins

Watercolour of *Oxalis*, painted in India, c1930.

Elaine returns

Monday 01

Tuesday 02

Wednesday 03

Thursday 04

New moon

Friday 05

Saturday 06

Sunday 07

Watercolour of *Nymphaea* or India lotus, painted in India, c1930.

APRIL

08 *Monday*

09 *Tuesday*

10 *Wednesday*

11 *Thursday*

12 *Friday*   *First quarter*

13 *Saturday*

14 *Sunday*   Palm Sunday

Watercolour of *Oxalis*, painted in India, c1930.

APRIL

Monday 15

Tuesday 16

Wednesday 17

Maundy Thursday

Thursday 18

Full moon
Good Friday
Holiday, UK, Canada, Australia and New Zealand

Friday 19

First day of Passover (Pesach)

Saturday 20

Easter Sunday
Birthday of Queen Elizabeth II

Sunday 21

Watercolour of *Oxalis corniculata*, Indian penny wood or creeping wood sorrel, painted in India, c1930.

APRIL

22 Monday

Easter Monday
Holiday, UK (exc. Scotland), Republic
of Ireland, Australia and New Zealand

23 Tuesday

St George's Day

24 Wednesday

25 Thursday

Holiday, Australia and New Zealand
(Anzac Day)

26 Friday

Last quarter

27 Saturday

28 Sunday

Watercolour of *Hesperantha coccinea* or crimson flag lily, previously known as
Schizostylis coccinea, painted in India, c1930.

Monday 29

Tuesday 30

Wednesday 01

Thursday 02

Friday 03

New moon

Saturday 04

Sunday 05

Watercolour of *Aerides ringens*, previously known as *Aerides radicosum (A. radicosa)*. This small, epiphytic orchid typically grows on tree bark and is native to India. Painted in India, c1930.

MAY

---

06 *Monday*

Early Spring Bank Holiday, UK
Holiday, Republic of Ireland
First day of Ramadân
(subject to sighting of the moon)

---

07 *Tuesday*

---

08 *Wednesday*

---

09 *Thursday*

---

10 *Friday*

---

11 *Saturday*

---

12 *Sunday*

First quarter
Mother's Day, USA, Canada,
Australia and New Zealand

Watercolour of *Anemone vitifolia* (misnamed *Anemone vitifolium* by the artist), painted in Shimla, India, 1934.

MAY

Monday 13

Tuesday 14

Wednesday 15

Thursday 16

Friday 17

Full moon

Saturday 18

Sunday 19

Watercolour of *Cobaea scandens*, also known as the cup and saucer vine, painted in India, c1930.

MAY

---

20 *Monday*   Holiday, Canada (Victoria Day)

---

21 *Tuesday*

---

22 *Wednesday*

---

23 *Thursday*

---

24 *Friday*

---

25 *Saturday*

---

26 *Sunday*   *Last quarter*

Watercolour of *Crotalaria* or Indian hemp, painted in India, c1930.

MAY/JUNE

Spring Bank Holiday, UK
Holiday, USA (Memorial Day)

Monday 27

Tuesday 28

Wednesday 29

Ascension Day

Thursday 30

Friday 31

Saturday 01

Coronation Day

Sunday 02

Watercolour of *Ipomoea indica* or blue dawn flower, previously known as *Ipomoea learii*, painted in India, c1930.

JUNE

---

03 Monday

New moon
Holiday, Republic of Ireland
Holiday, New Zealand (The Queen's Birthday)

---

04 Tuesday

---

05 Wednesday

Eid al-Fitr (end of Ramadân)
(subject to sighting of the moon)

---

06 Thursday

---

07 Friday

---

08 Saturday

The Queen's Official Birthday
(subject to confirmation)

---

09 Sunday

Whit Sunday
Feast of Weeks (Shavuot)

Watercolour of mixed *Cannas*, also known as canna lilies or Indian shot, painted in India, 1930s.

JUNE

First quarter
Holiday, Australia (The Queen's Birthday)

Monday 10

Tuesday 11

Wednesday 12

Thursday 13

Friday 14

Saturday 15

Trinity Sunday
Father's Day, UK, Republic of Ireland,
USA and Canada

Sunday 16

Watercolour of *Aerides ringens*, painted in Ootacamund, southern India, 1933.

JUNE

---

17 Monday   *Full moon*

---

18 Tuesday

---

19 Wednesday

---

20 Thursday   Corpus Christi

---

21 Friday   Summer Solstice (Summer begins)

---

22 Saturday

---

23 Sunday

Watercolour of *Barleria cristata*, painted in India, c1930.

JUNE

Monday 24

Last quarter

Tuesday 25

Wednesday 26

Thursday 27

Friday 28

Saturday 29

Sunday 30

Watercolour of *Albizia julibrissin* f. *rosea* or pink silk tree, painted in India, c1930.

JULY

---

01 Monday   Holiday, Canada (Canada Day)

---

02 Tuesday   New moon

---

03 Wednesday

---

04 Thursday   Holiday, USA (Independence Day)

---

05 Friday

---

06 Saturday

---

07 Sunday

Watercolour of *Bauhinia purpurea* or butterfly tree, painted in Madras, India, c1930.

JULY

Monday 08

First quarter

Tuesday 09

Wednesday 10

Thursday 11

Holiday, Northern Ireland (Battle of the Boyne)

Friday 12

Saturday 13

Sunday 14

Watercolour of *Barleria involucrata* var. *elata*, now thought to be *B. cristata*, painted in India, c1930.

JULY

15 *Monday*   St Swithin's Day

16 *Tuesday*   *Full moon*

17 *Wednesday*

18 *Thursday*

19 *Friday*

20 *Saturday*

21 *Sunday*

Watercolour of *Hibiscus*, painted in Madras, India, c1930.

Monday 22

Tuesday 23

Wednesday 24

Last quarter

Thursday 25

Friday 26

Saturday 27

Sunday 28

Watercolour of *Cassia didymobotrya* or golden wonder, painted in India, c1930.

JULY/AUGUST

29 *Monday*

30 *Tuesday*

31 *Wednesday*

01 *Thursday*   *New moon*

02 *Friday*

03 *Saturday*

04 *Sunday*

Watercolour of *Brownea grandiceps* or rose of Venezuela and *Brownea coccinea* × *latifolia*, previously known as *Brownea coccinea*, painted in India, c1930.

Brownea coccinea.

Brownea grandiceps

Holiday, Scotland and Republic of Ireland

Monday 05

Tuesday 06

First quarter

Wednesday 07

Thursday 08

Friday 09

Saturday 10

Sunday 11

Watercolour of *Bignonia magnifica*, painted in India, c1930.

AUGUST

12 Monday

13 Tuesday

14 Wednesday

15 Thursday   *Full moon*

16 Friday

17 Saturday

18 Sunday

Watercolour of *Butea monosperma*, commonly known as flame of the forest, previously known as *Butea frondosa*, painted in India, c1930.

AUGUST

Monday 19

Tuesday 20

Wednesday 21

Thursday 22

Last quarter

Friday 23

Saturday 24

Sunday 25

Watercolour of *Calanthe triplicata*, previously known as *Calanthe veratrifolia*. This orchid is commonly found in southern India. Painted in India, c1930.

AUGUST/SEPTEMBER

---

26 *Monday*   Summer Bank Holiday, UK (exc. Scotland)

---

27 *Tuesday*

---

28 *Wednesday*

---

29 *Thursday*

---

30 *Friday*   *New moon*

---

31 *Saturday*

---

01 *Sunday*   Islamic New Year
Father's Day, Australia and New Zealand

Watercolour of *Caesalpinia pulcherrima*, painted in Madras, India, c1930.

SEPTEMBER

Holiday, USA (Labor Day)
Holiday, Canada (Labour Day)

Monday 02

Tuesday 03

Wednesday 04

Thursday 05

First quarter

Friday 06

Saturday 07

Sunday 08

Watercolour of *Senna auriculata* or avaram, it was previously known as *Cassia auriculata*.
Painted in India, c1930.

SEPTEMBER

09 *Monday*

10 *Tuesday*

11 *Wednesday*

12 *Thursday*

13 *Friday*

14 *Saturday*   *Full moon*

15 *Sunday*

Watercolour of *Calotropis gigantea* or Indian bowstring hemp, painted in India, c1930.

SEPTEMBER

Monday 16

Tuesday 17

Wednesday 18

Thursday 19

Friday 20

Saturday 21

Last quarter

Sunday 22

Watercolour of *Barleria cristata rosea* and *Barleria strigosa*, found growing in the foothills of the Himalayas. Painted in India, c1930.

SEPTEMBER

23 *Monday*   Autumnal Equinox (Autumn begins)

24 *Tuesday*

25 *Wednesday*

26 *Thursday*

27 *Friday*

28 *Saturday*   *New moon*

29 *Sunday*   Michaelmas Day

Watercolour of *Couroupita guianensis* or cannonball tree, painted in India, c1930.

SEPTEMBER/OCTOBER

Jewish New Year (Rosh Hashanah)   Monday 30

Tuesday 01

Wednesday 02

Thursday 03

Friday 04

First quarter   Saturday 05

Sunday 06

Watercolour of *Cochlospermum gossypium*, painted in India, c1930.

OCTOBER

07 Monday

08 Tuesday

09 Wednesday   Day of Atonement (Yom Kippur)

10 Thursday

11 Friday

12 Saturday

13 Sunday   *Full moon*

Watercolour of *Fagraea obovata*, painted in India, c1930.

OCTOBER

First day of Tabernacles (Succoth)
Holiday, USA (Columbus Day)
Holiday, Canada (Thanksgiving)

Monday 14

Tuesday 15

Wednesday 16

Thursday 17

Friday 18

Saturday 19

Sunday 20

Watercolour of *Gliricidia sepium* or madre de cacao/mother of cocoa, previously known as *Gliricidia maculata*, painted in Madras, India, c1930.

OCTOBER

---

21 Monday   *Last quarter*

---

22 Tuesday

---

23 Wednesday

---

24 Thursday

---

25 Friday

---

26 Saturday

---

27 Sunday   British Summer Time ends

Watercolour of *Beaumontia grandiflora* or Nepal trumpet flower, painted in Madras, India, c1930.

OCTOBER/NOVEMBER

New moon
Holiday, Republic of Ireland
Holiday, New Zealand (Labour Day)

Monday 28

Tuesday 29

Wednesday 30

Halloween

Thursday 31

All Saints' Day

Friday 01

Saturday 02

Sunday 03

Watercolour of *Digitalis canariensis*, previously known as *Isoplexis canariensis*, originally from the Canary Islands. Painted in India, c1930.

NOVEMBER

04 Monday   *First quarter*

05 Tuesday   Guy Fawkes

06 Wednesday

07 Thursday

08 Friday

09 Saturday

10 Sunday   Remembrance Sunday

Watercolour of *Datura sanguinea*, painted in Ootacamund, India, c1930.

NOVEMBER

Holiday, USA (Veterans Day)
Holiday, Canada (Remembrance Day)

Monday 11

Full moon

Tuesday 12

Wednesday 13

Thursday 14

Friday 15

Saturday 16

Sunday 17

Watercolour of *Lagerstroemia indica* or crape myrtle, painted in India, c1930.

NOVEMBER

18 Monday

19 Tuesday

Last quarter

20 Wednesday

21 Thursday

22 Friday

23 Saturday

24 Sunday

Watercolour of *Ochna squarrosa* or golden champak, painted in India, c1930.

NOVEMBER/DECEMBER

Monday 25

New moon

Tuesday 26

Wednesday 27

Holiday, USA (Thanksgiving)

Thursday 28

Friday 29

St Andrew's Day

Saturday 30

First Sunday in Advent

Sunday 01

Watercolour of *Phaedranassa aurantiaca*, now identified as *Stenomesson miniatum*, painted in India, c1930.

DECEMBER

02 Monday

03 Tuesday

04 Wednesday   *First quarter*

05 Thursday

06 Friday

07 Saturday

08 Sunday

Watercolour of *Prunus cerasoides* or wild Himalayan cherry, previously known as
Prunus puddum, painted in India, c1930.

DECEMBER

Monday 09

Tuesday 10

Wednesday 11

Full moon

Thursday 12

Friday 13

Saturday 14

Sunday 15

Watercolour of canna lilies, painted in India, 1930s.

DECEMBER

---

16 Monday

---

17 Tuesday

---

18 Wednesday

---

19 Thursday   *Last quarter*

---

20 Friday

---

21 Saturday

---

22 Sunday   Winter Solstice (Winter begins)
                                                 Hannukah begins (at sunset)

Watercolour of *Salvia involucrata* 'Bethellii' or rosy-leaf sage, previously known
as *Salvia bethellii*, painted in India, c1930.

DECEMBER

Monday 23

Christmas Eve

Tuesday 24

Christmas Day
Holiday, UK, Republic of Ireland,
USA, Canada, Australia and New Zealand

Wednesday 25

New moon
Boxing Day (St Stephen's Day)
Holiday, UK, Republic of Ireland,
Canada, Australia and New Zealand

Thursday 26

Friday 27

Saturday 28

Sunday 29

Watercolour of *Kigelia pinnata* or sausage tree, painted in India, c1930.

DECEMBER/JANUARY WEEK 01/2020

30 *Monday*
Hannukah ends

31 *Tuesday*
New Year's Eve

01 *Wednesday*
New Year's Day
Holiday, UK, Republic of Ireland, USA,
Canada, Australia and New Zealand

02 *Thursday*
Holiday, Scotland and New Zealand

03 *Friday*

04 *Saturday*

05 *Sunday*

Watercolour on paper of *Zantedeschia aethiopica* or calla lily, previously known as *Richardia africana*, painted in India, 1930s.

YEAR PLANNER

JANUARY	JULY
FEBRUARY	AUGUST
MARCH	SEPTEMBER
APRIL	OCTOBER
MAY	NOVEMBER
JUNE	DECEMBER